SWU-MED-002

HEIDELBERG TURNIERBUCH 1482

Luca Stefano Cristini

SOLDIERSHOP PUBLISHING

NOTE ABOUT BOOK PRINTING BEFORE 1925

This book may contain text or images coming from a reproduction of a book published before 1925 (over seventy years ago). No effort has been made to modernize or standardize the spelling used in the original text, so this book may have occasional imperfections such as missing or blurred pages, poor pictures, errant marks, etc. that were either part of the original artifact, or were introduced by the scanning process. We believe this work is culturally important, and despite the imperfections, have elected to bring it back into print (digital and/or paper) as part of our continuing commitment to the preservation of printed works worldwide. We appreciate your understanding of the imperfections in the preservation process, and hope you enjoy this valuable book. Now this book is purpose re-built and is proof-read and re-type set from the original to provide an outstanding experience of reflowing text, also for an ebook reader. However Soldiershop publishing added, enriched, revised and overhauled the text, images, etc. of the cover and the book. Therefore, the job is now to all intents and purposes a derivative work, and the added, new and original parts of the book are the copyright of Soldiershop. On this second unpublished part of the book none of images or text may be reproduced in any format without the expressed written permission of Soldiershop. Almost many of the images of our books and prints are taken from original first edition prints or books that are no longer in copyright and are therefore public domain. We have been a specialized bookstore for a long time so we (and several friends antiquarian booksellers) have readily available a lot of ancient, historical and illustrated books not in copyright. Each of our prints, art designs or illustrations is either our own creation, or a fully digitally restoration by our computer artists, or non copyrighted images. All of our prints are "tagged" with a registered digital copyright. Soldiershop remains to disposition of the possible having right for all the doubtful sources images or not identifies.

LICENSES COMMONS

This book could utilize material marked with license creative commons 3.0 or 4.0 (CC BY 4.0), (CC BY-ND 4.0), (CC BY-SA 4.0) or (CC0 1.0). In this case We give appropriate attribution credit and indicate if change were made below in the acknowledgements field.

ACKNOWLEDGEMENTS

A Special Thanks to the Heidelberg University Library for their kindly permission to use several images of his collections used in the book.

Title: **HEIDELBERG TURNIERBUCH 1482**
By Luca Stefano Cristini.   First edition December 2016 by Soldiershop.
Cover & Art Design: Luca S. Cristini & Matteo Radaelli   ISBN code: 978-88-93271769

Published by Soldiershop publishing, via Padre Davide, 7 - 24050 Zanica (BG) ITALY. www.soldiershop.com

HEIDELBERG
TURNIERBUCH
1482

XIXth century print related the world of medieval tournament.

PREFACE

The Manuscript of Heidelberg Tournament Book of the Jost Pirckhammer

This German manuscript Turnierbuch is a falsification of the *"Heidelberg Tournament Book of the Jost Pirckhammer of 1486"* realized in 1886. Today it is preserved in Heidelberg University Library.

Always and in any time, people were fascinated by the Middle Ages. And as always, writings and other legacies from the Middle Ages were an expensive and coveted commodity. And where there was a need for rare originals, there were always a "creative contemporaries" who were able to recreate old originals... In appendix twelve plates o knights, dames ans soldiers of XVIth century.

ITALIAN TEXT:

La storia di questo manoscritto è davvero curiosa. Il Turnierbuch di Heidelberg attribuito a Jost Pirckhammer del 1486 non è un originale. Si tratta infatti di una elaborazione falsaria della prima metà dell'ottocento. Realizzata cercando di mantenre lo stile proprio dei turnierbuch rinascimentali ma tratendo in molte parti quella caratteristica oleografica di primo ottocento. Eppure negli anni della sua scoperta questo artefatto trasse in inganno un "esperto" collezionista tedesco che acquistò il libro per una montagna di sterline presso un antiquario londinese... In appendice dodici tavole di cavalieri, soldati e dame del XVI secolo

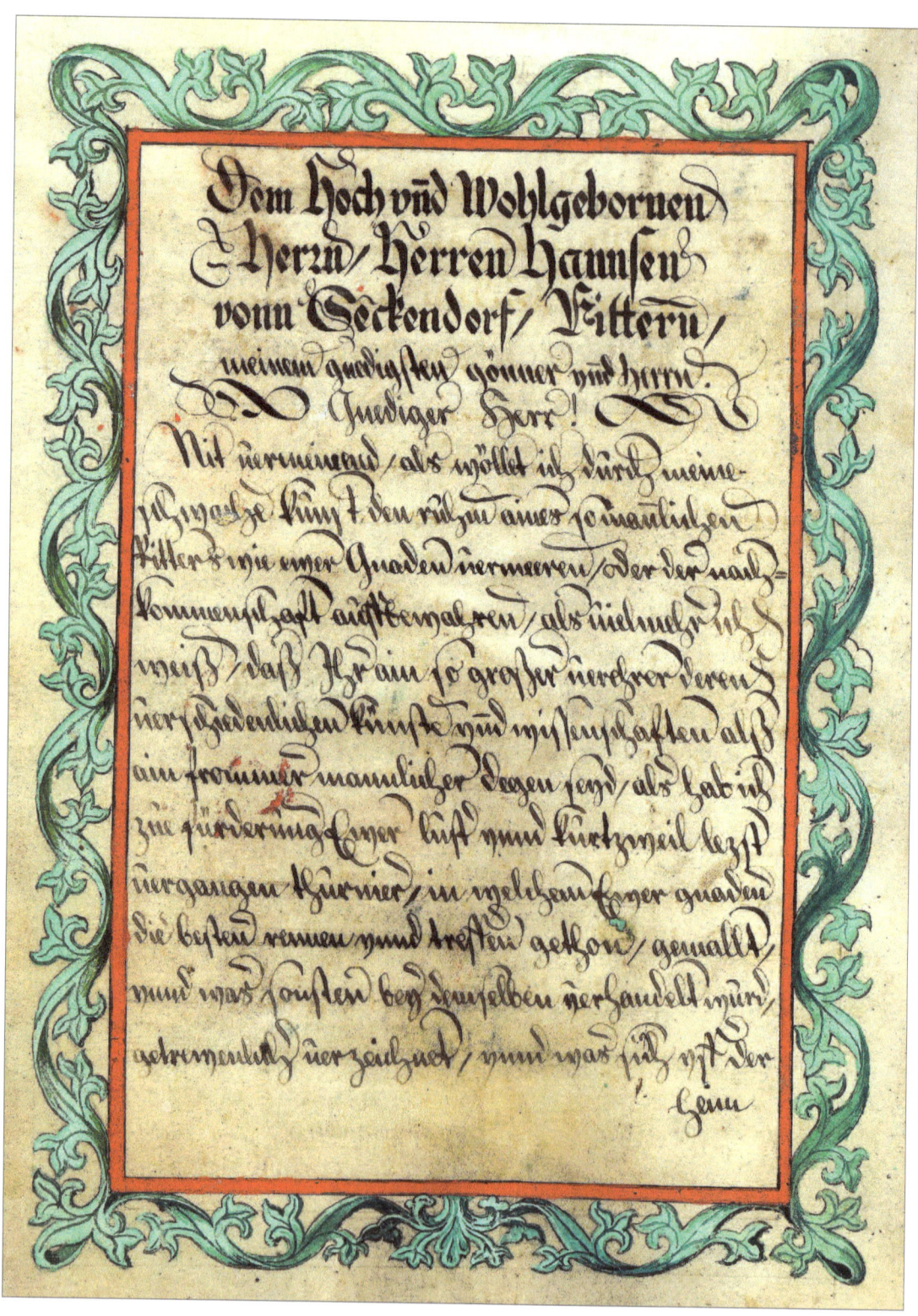

Fronspiece of the manuscript of Heidelberg

THE MANUSCRIPT OF HEIDELBERG TOURNAMENT BOOK OF THE JOST PIRCKHAMMER

This German manuscript Turnierbuch is a falsification of the "Heidelberg Tournament Book of the Jost Pirckhammer of 1486" realized in 1886. Always and in any time, people were fascinated by the Middle Ages. And as always, writings and other legacies from the Middle Ages were an expensive and coveted commodity. And where there was a need for rare originals, there were always a "creative contemporaries" who were able to recreate old originals. Thus in August 1868, Albert Mays, a German collector and founder of the Heidelberger urban antiquities collection, acquired the "Heidelberger Turnierbuch des Jost Pirckhammer von 1486" in London. He probably gave a considerable sum for to buy this work. The pastor Hermann Wirth inform us that in 1868 this Heidelberg tournament was moved in his "Archives of the History of the City of Heidelberg". After, in late XIX century, two german scientists: Marc Rosenberg first, and the Berliner Verein "Herold" after unmasked the work as falsification. The heraldic Theodor Wickens published the investigation result of the association in 1900 under the title "The" Heidelberger Thurnierbuch and Order of the Jost Pirckhammer of 1486 is a fake". It is probably that the forger to have produced the work around the first half of XIX century and reused it for the production of parchment from the 18th century. Also the tournament book of the herald Georg Rüxner from the year 1530 should have served as a text-file. Again the portrait of Elector Philip came from a portrait book by Jost Amman. Today, this wrong "mediaeval" work, with its beautiful illustrations, is now preserved in the Heidelberg University Library.

The Contents

Usually this book is unique in several aspects, compared to other original medieval German turnier books. The original manuscript is composed of 63 pages, some text and most illustrations. In our reproduction we have given up the text parts to enhance as much as possible the beautiful color plates. In addition we also recolored some tables were present in monochrome.

One unique feature is the drawings of tournaments in which servants and peasants took part, thus demonstrating the more popular entertainment, which came to accompany what was the more traditional elements of tournaments – jousting and fighting.

Our Tournament book has been faithfully edited and accompanied with careful explanations of what is seen in the different drawings.

GLOSSARY OF GERMAN TERMS ABOUT TURNIERBUCH

Ablaufen - running off
Abnehmen - taking off
Abschneiden - cutting off
Absetzen - setting off
Ansetzen - setting on
Duplieren - doubling
Durchgehen / geh durch - go through
Durchwechseln / wechsel durch - change through
Durchlaufen / lauf durch - running through
Eber - guard position, "boar"
Einlaufen - running in
Entrüsthau - hidden strike, "disarming strike"
Geferhau - hidden strike, "danger strike"
Hängen - hanging
Halbhau - "half strike"
Indes - simultaneously, instantly
Langes Messer - long knife
Luginsland - guard position, "look over the land"
Messer - knife
Messernehmen - taking the Messer
Mordschlag - strike with the pommel
Mutieren - mutating
Nachreißen - jerking after
Oberhau - strike from above
Pastei - guard position, "bastion"
Pnehmen / pnimm - removing(?)
Pogen - arc / bow
Schrankhut - "barrier guard"
Sonnenzeigen - showing the sun
Stier - guard position, "bull"
Überlaufen / lauf über - running over
Unterhau - strike from below
Wecker - hidden strike, "wakener"
Winden - winding
Winker - hidden strike, "waver"
Zornhau - hidden strike, "wrath strike"
Zornhau-Ort - Zornhau-point
Zucken - jerking / snatching
Zufechten - approaching in fencing / getting into striking distance / engagement
Zwinger - hidden strike, "forcer"

IL MANOSCRITTO DEL LIBRO DEL TORNEO DI HEIDELBERG DI JOST PIRCKHAMMER

Questo manoscritto tedesco, (deutsch Turnierbuch) è in realtà un noto falso. Conosciuto col Nome di "Heidelberg Turnierbuch von of Jost Pirckhammer 1486" esso fu in realtà realizzato nella prima metà dell'ottocento

Sempre ed in ogni tempo la gente si è appassionata di quanto concerne il mondo e le storie medievali . E di conseguenza si è sempre attivata una passione collezionistica per oggetti e libri del periodo. Oggetti rari e preziosi, e in mancanza di essi si è sempre trovato qualche "creativo" in grado di realizzare ottimi "originali".

Fu così che nell'estate del 1868, Albert Mays, un collezionista tedesco e fondatore dell'associazione *Heidelberger urban antiquities collection*, acquistò presso un antiquario londinese il manoscritto *"Heidelberger Turnierbuch des Jost Pirckhammer von 1486"*. E' molto probabile che il collezionista abbia pagato lo stesso manoscritto un vero sproposito, visto che gli era stato presentato come un originale del tardo '400.

Tempo dopo il pastore tedesco Hermann Wirth notificava la presenza di tale manoscritto nell'archivio di storia della città di Heidelberg nel Palatinato.

Infine verso la fine del secolo XIX due eminenti studiosi: Marc Rosenberg prima, e il berlinese Verein "Herold" decretarono al di là di ogni ragionevole dubbio che il manoscritto del tardo quattrocento era per lo meno più giovane di almeno quattro secoli. Lo studioso di araldica Theodor Wickens pubblicò i resoconti di tali investigazioni nel 1900 presso gli archivi dell'associazione sotto il titolo di "Il turnierbuch di Heidelberg del 1486 attribuito a Jost Pirckhammer of 1486 è in realtà un falso apocrifo".

Risultò indicata la prima metà dell'ottocento come data possibile nella realizzazione del manufatto da parte del falsario il quale utilizzò per tale "misfatto" delle pergamene del '700.. Per il resto egli sfruttò in maniera certosina per il testo il ricco manuale del mitico Georg Rüxner datato attorno al 1530.

Manuale di sicuro riferimento per quanto riguarda la storia dei tornei medievali specialmente di quelli di area tedesca.

Pare certo che per il ritratto dell'elettore palatino fu utilizzata una copia derivata da un libro di Jost Amman.

Oggi questo discusso ma bellissimo manoscritto è conservato presso la Heidelberg University Library.

Il contenuto

Nonostante si tratti di un falso, questo libro rimane comunque unico per molti diversi aspetti. Esso è composto Da 63 pagine, la maggior parte di esse illustrate con colori vividi assai suggestivi.

Nella nostra edizione diverse tavole che nell'originale erano seppiate sono state ricolorate alla stessa maniera di quelle a tutto colore già presenti.

Le scene sono tipiche di quelle dei Turnierbuch originali (il falsario ci sapeva fare..)

Scene di torneo con dame e cavalieri, paesani e serventi, araldi e altro che tutti insieme prendono parte a questi intrattenimenti popolari di un certo successo.

In appendice abbiamo aggiunto dodici tavole di cavalieri, dame e soldati del 1543.

Three renaissance engraving on tournament by Lucas Cranach.

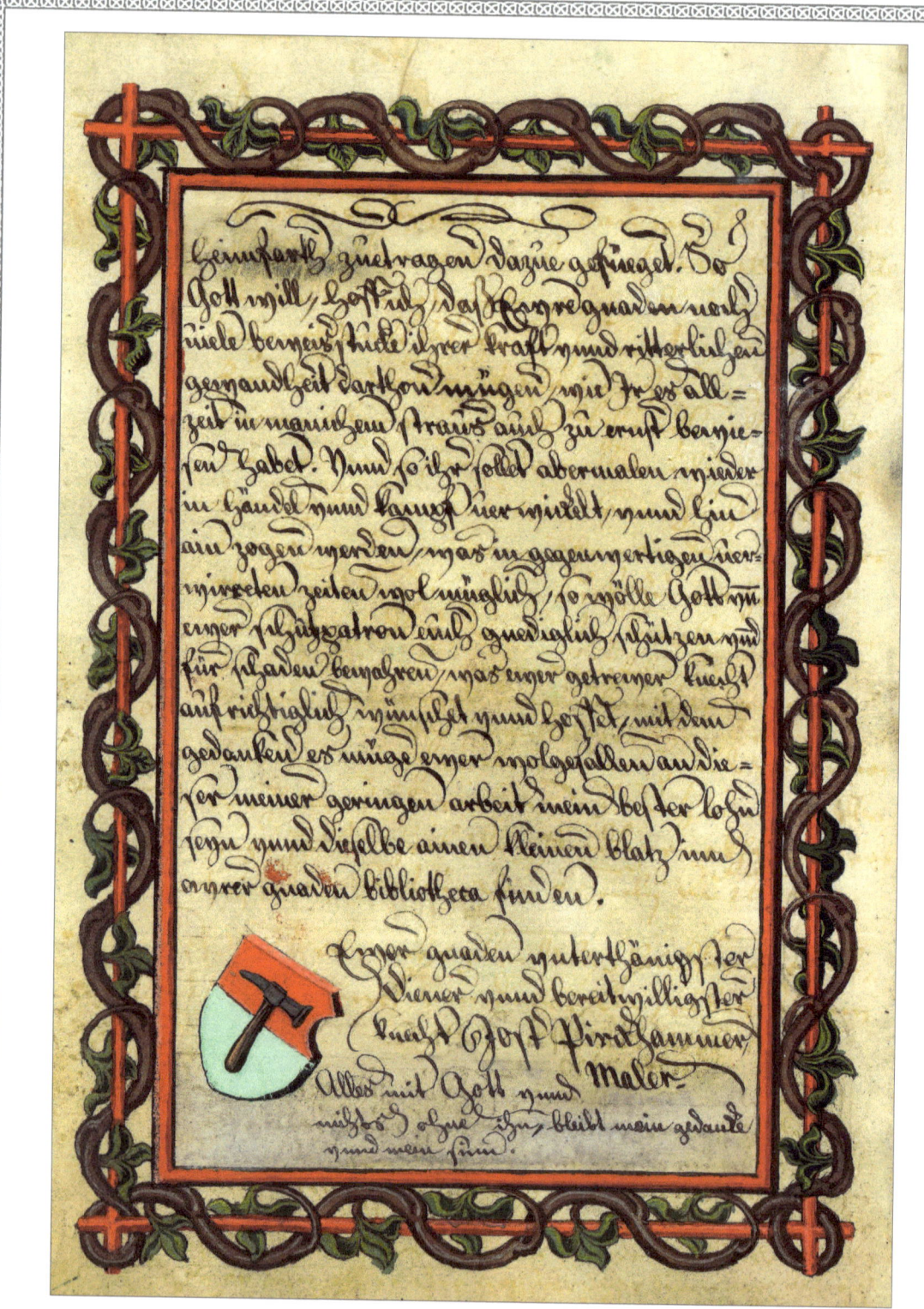

heimfarth zugetragen dazue gefüeget. So
Gott will, hoff ich, daß Eure gnaden noch
viele der ihres khind ihrer kraft ynud ritterlichen
gehandheit dartton mögen, wie Er es all=
zeit in manchem straus auch zu erst berzie=
ren habet. Unnd so ihr sollt abermalen wieder
in handel ynud kampff hier wirklet, ynud hin
ain zogen werden, was in gegenwärtigen ver=
wirreten zeiten wol müglich, so wölle Gott ym
euer schutzpatron euch gnediglich schützen ynud
für schaden bewahren, was euer getreuer knecht
aufrichtiglich wünschet ynud bettet, mit dem
gedanken es möge euer wolgefallen an die=
ser meiner geringen arbeit mein bester lohn
seyn ynud dieselbe ainen kleinen blatz inn
eurer gnaden bibliotheca finden.

Euer gnaden underthänigster
Diener ynud bereitwilligster
knecht Jost Pirckhammer
Maler.
Alles mit Gott ynud
nichts ohne Ihn, bleibt mein gedanck
ynud mein sinn.

Portrait of Hans von Gessendorf

Portrait of a noble woman of Palatine court

Portrait of the Count Palatine

Portrait of a noble German knight (Gessendorf ?)

Portrait of the noble German standard bearer

Portrait of a noble German knight

Coat of Arms of various noble family of Palatine

Coat of arm of the city of Heidelberg

leave letters for the knights

The beginning of the tournament celebrations

Clash of knights

Clash of knights

Clash of knights

Clash of knights

Mein gnediger Herr.   Der Herr von Penckwitzug.

Clash of knights at foot

The dressing Knight

Clash of knights

Clash of knights

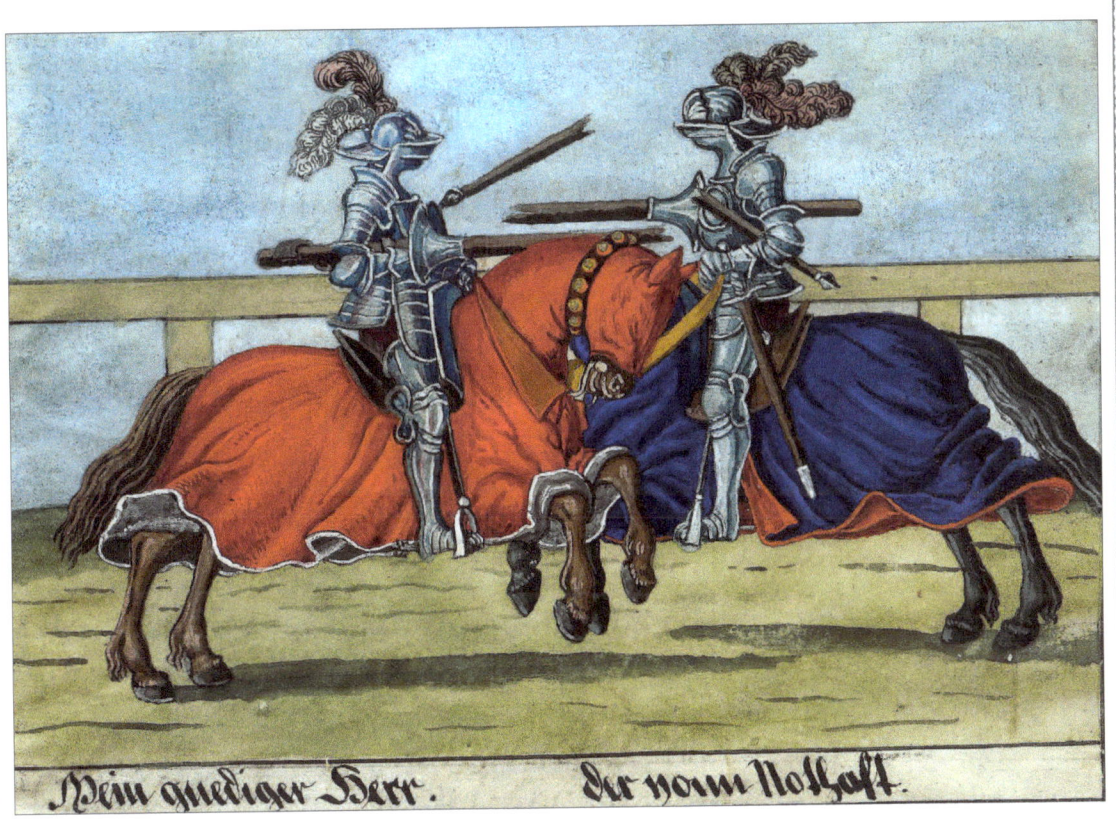

Clash of knights

Clash of knights

The delivery of the helmets to the Knights

The ring of knights tournament

Servants, soldiers and paesants of Heidelberg

Knights attacked by the brigands

The Lady and Knight (the courtly love)

Knights at horse in Burgkmair style

Knights at horse in Burgkmair style

Knights at horse in Burgkmair style

Knights at horse in Burgkmair style

Knights at horse in Burgkmair style

Knights at horse in Burgkmair style

Knights at horse in Burgkmair style

Knights at horse in ancient dress style

Knights at horse in Burgkmair style

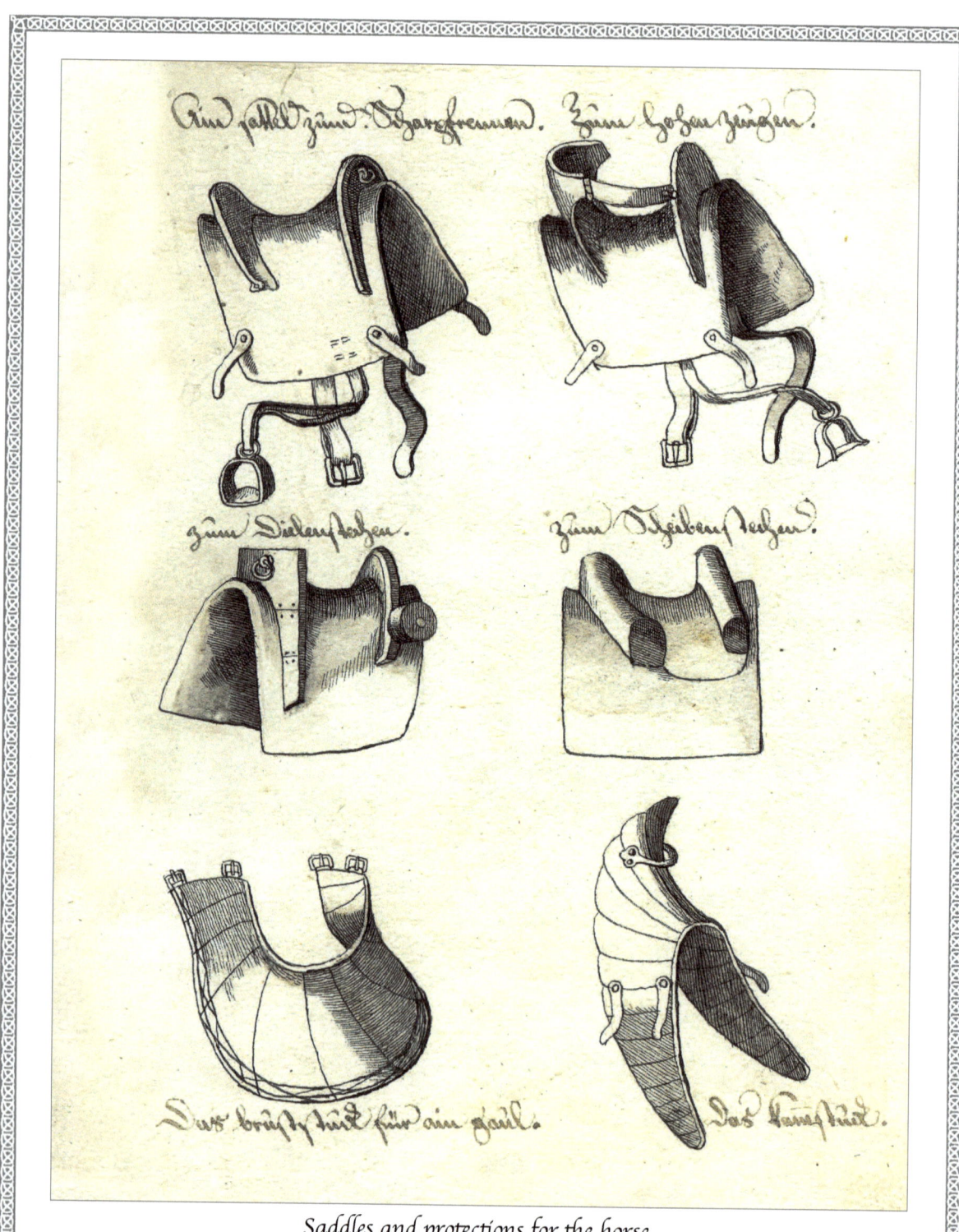

Saddles and protections for the horse

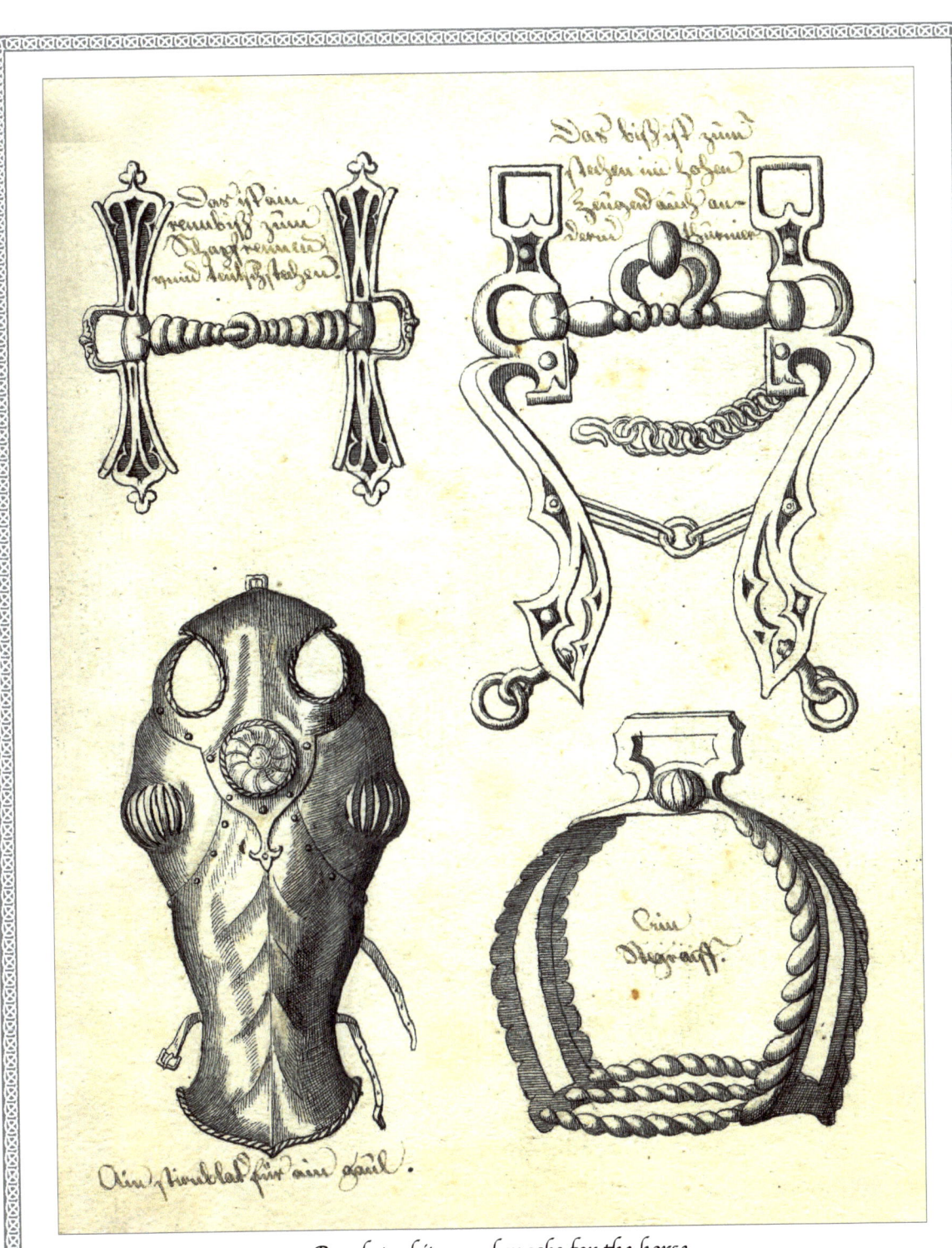

Brackets, bites and masks for the horse

49

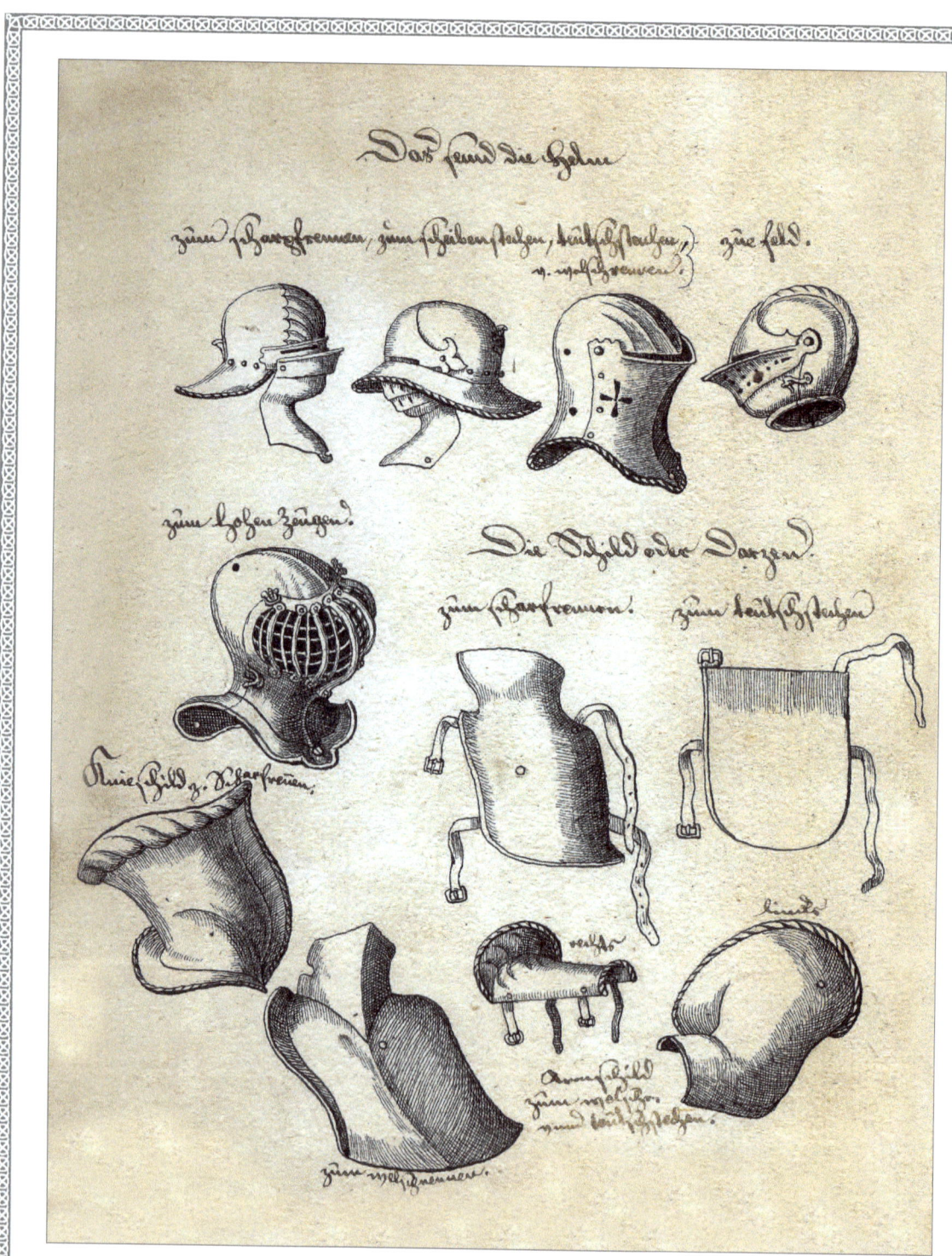

Helmets and cuirass

APPENDIX
LATE
MEDIEVAL KNIGKTS
IN CITY DRESS

Johannes Herzog of Sax 1518

a   *b*

Two knight in 1519

a   b

Two knight in winter dress in 1521

a
b

A crossbowman and a servants in 1521

a   *b*

Two soldies in winter dress 1521

A captain and an halberdier with helmet in 1521

Communal militia, heavy infantryman XIII century

Communal militia, death's company 1176

a   b

Two knight in 1521

a　　　　　　　　　*b*

Two knight in winter dress in 1521

Koningin Anna Catherine of Brandenburg 1575

Anna María von Neuburg 1620

SOLDIERS, WEAPONS & UNIFORMS ALREADY PUBLISHED

At now in the paper books serie of **Soldiers, weapons & Uniforms** we have printed the first part of Viskovatov's work dedicated to the uniforms and weapons belonging to the Russian army during the Napoleonic period, until 1825. And a book on Austrian army from XVII century to XIX century.

Our new edition, the first ever published in English, both on paper and digital format, boasts a large number of color plates, many of them unpublished and colored by our team of expert artists of uniformology. Each volume is based on several color plates, always accompanied by the original translated text which describes the uniforms, the organization and the armament of the subjects.

 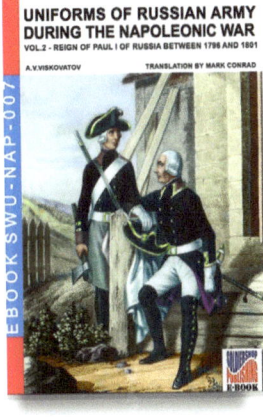  

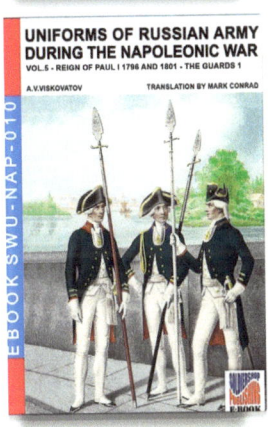 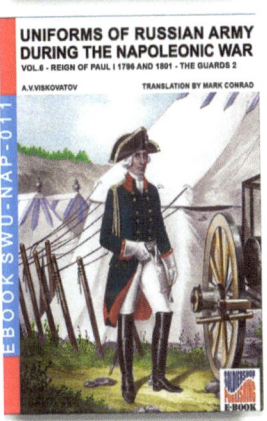 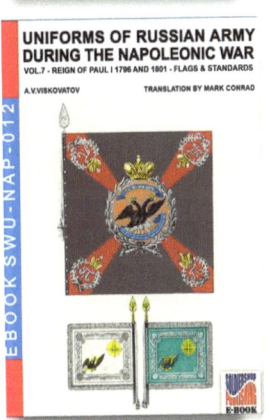 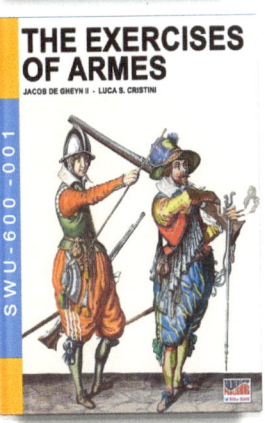

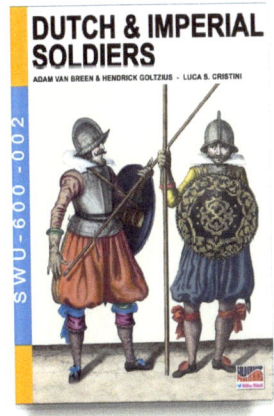  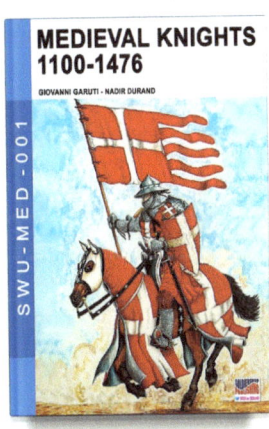